GUIDELINES

Praying
for the Sick

Dr. Marilyn Neubauer

*Now thanks be to God
who always leads us in triumph in Christ,
and through us diffuses the fragrance of
His knowledge in every place.*

2 Corinthians 2:14 NKJV

Triumphant Living

Praying
for the Sick

Dr. Marilyn Neubauer

Christian Literature & Artwork
A BOLD TRUTH Publication

Guidelines - Praying for the Sick

Copyright © 2016 by Marilyn Neubauer Ministries
Revised Version Copyright © 2018
ISBN 13: 978-0-9998051-9-0

Marilyn Neubauer Ministries
P.O. Box 4664 ▪ Oceanside, CA 92052
www.marilynneubauer.com

BOLD TRUTH PUBLISHING
(Christian Literature & Artwork)
606 West 41st, Ste. 4
Sand Springs, Oklahoma 74063
www.BoldTruthPublishing.com ▪ *beirep@yahoo.com*

Available from Amazon.com and other retail outlets.
Quantity discount orders are available through
marilynneubauer.com

Printed in the USA.
1018   10 9 8 7 6 5 4 3 2 1

Table of Contents

Triumphant Living

Personal Coaching

*As a lighthouse is to a lost ship at sea guiding her to the shore,
I am here to guide you into the light of God's Word
and bring you to a place of divine healing.*

*You will also declare a thing, And it will be established for you;
So light will shine on your ways. Job 22:28*

To receive information on my personal coaching
program for healing, email:
marilynneubauer@gmail.com

Dr. Marilyn Neubauer

Introduction

Ambassadors for Christ

Over the years I have prayed for numerous people who were sick and I've seen many miracles. I prayed for those in the healing line at church and others in their home or hospital, but I have also been on the other side of the hospital bed. I've tasted the depth of pain accompanied by the thoughts the pain itself could kill me before the disease would. Pain medication helps, but it takes about an hour for it to take effect. It usually lasts about two hours and then wears off. Following that, you are in pain once more for about an hour before it's time for more medication. Once again the cycle begins. So then, during a period of four hours, you only have two hours of pain relief.

Therefore, I *knew* that it would be another two hours before relief came. I have lain in bed making no complaints to the nurse, but had tears stream down my face. I'd pray, *"God, please stop this pain!"*

When I was young in the Lord I didn't understand my authority as a believer (Luke 10:19) nor how to *speak to the mountain* (Mark 11:23) of pain I was experiencing. I would plead to God for help instead of knowing how to be strong in applying the Word of God.

1

Introduction

Behold, I have given you authority to trample on serpents and scorpions, and over all the power of the enemy, and nothing shall by any means hurt you.

Luke 10:19 NKJV

I'm sharing these guidelines to encourage you that it is a God-ordained honor to pray for the sick. When you pray, do it with a heart of compassion - not with pity, but with compassion. Not everyone you pray for will be on the same level of faith as you, but let the love of God come forth. Sometimes just knowing someone cares can strengthen one's faith. Be sensitive to their pain, agony and fear. As a vessel of honor, pray with boldness and with your God-given authority, being fully persuaded by the Words of the Lord, *"they shall recover" (Mark 16:15-18).*

Perhaps you've asked yourself if you qualify to pray for the sick. If you're a believer, you qualify.

Therefore, if anyone is in Christ, he is a new creation; old things have passed away; behold, all things have become new. Now all things are of God, who has reconciled us to Himself through Jesus Christ, and has given us the ministry of reconciliation, that is, that God was in Christ reconciling the world to Himself, not imputing their trespasses to them, and has committed to us the word of reconciliation. Now then, we are ambassadors for Christ, as though God were pleading through us: we implore you on Christ's behalf, be reconciled to God.

2 Corinthians 5:17-20

This is a high-ranking position in the Kingdom of God. The word *ambassador* can be defined as: a diplomatic agent of the highest rank authorized to speak on behalf of his sender. What an honor it is be a voice from Heaven sharing His heart of compassion in reconciling a lost and hurting world back to God, the Father.

The Great Commission is not the Great Suggestion. As Ambassadors for Christ it's our God-given earthly appointment.

And He said to them, "Go into all the world and preach the gospel to every creature. He who believes and is baptized will be saved; but he who does not believe will be condemned. And these signs will follow those who believe: In My name they will cast out demons; they will speak with new tongues; they will take up serpents; and if they drink anything deadly, it will by no means hurt them; they will lay hands on the sick, and they will recover."

Mark 16:15-18 NKJV

The last word in this Scripture is *recover*. The meaning of the word *recover* is *to get better*. Most healings are in the form of recovery, not instant. But we can be confident that if we obey and lay hands on the sick as Jesus did, the healing power of God will attack the infirmity. God simply needs willing vessels. This is our responsibility as His Ambassadors.

The first miracle of Jesus was changing water into wine. However, His first miracle of healing was that of the Nobleman's son who began to amend, meaning he began to get better, not instantly healed *(John 4:46)*.

Jesus is the Healer, but we are the vessel through which His healing power flows. As we lay hands on the sick, it becomes a point of contact which can release their faith to receive. It's the healing power of God flowing from the believer to the one who is sick. It's the hand of the Lord being extended through our hands. Every believer can lay hands on the sick and expect to see them recover.

As Ambassadors for Christ, we do this in obedience to the Great Commission. We never have to wait for a feeling or goose bumps. Just simply obey the Word and the Lord will do His part. He is the Healer and we are the vessels. We are not responsible, however, if someone doesn't receive healing.

Chapter 1

Time of Preparation

According to the *Gospel of John*, Jesus makes it very clear that apart from Him we can do nothing. Therefore, to be effective as His Ambassadors, we must have vital union with Christ.

> *"I am the Vine; you are the branches. The one who remains in Me and I in him bears much fruit, for [otherwise] apart from Me [that is, cut off from vital union with Me] you can do nothing."*
>
> John 15:5 AMP

Having vital union with Him comes through intimacy. His presence brings an anointed outflow enabling us to bear much fruit as we pray for the sick. We don't want hit and miss results. We want to bear much fruit.

Some people needing prayer will have minor ailments and others will have been diagnosed with a terminal disease.

These precious people need our prayers whether they are Christians or not. In order for us to fulfill this assignment from the Lord, we must first set aside *a time of preparation.*

The key is to go forth with the anointing through the help of the Holy Spirit.

> *And I will ask the Father, and He will give you another Helper (Comforter, Advocate, Intercessor—Counselor, Strengthener, Standby), to be with you forever.*
> John 14:16 AMP

I want to emphasize three words from this Scripture.

▶ ANOTHER - this word means, *one of the same kind.* Jesus is saying, what I have been to you, the Holy Spirit will now be to you One of the same kind.

If you were in a restaurant and had a delicious slice of apple pie and then asked the waitress for another slice, she would know you want one of the same kind, not a slice of pecan pie.

▶ COUNSELOR - when praying for the sick, the Holy Spirit within is able to give us counsel as to the specific need of the individual. Rather than needing an actual healing, perhaps an adjustment in the person's diet is all that is needed.

I had a minister friend who became ill and he prayed seeking counsel as to what was causing the negative symptoms in His body. Through the counsel of the Holy Spirit he was given insight that his body was lacking salt. As soon as he responded to this insight from the Holy Spirit and increased his salt intake, he recovered quickly. There was no need to see the doctor or take medication.

▶ HELPER - He is the Revealer of Mysteries.

For he who speaks in a tongue does not speak to men, but to God, for no one understands him; however, in the spirit he speaks mysteries.
                                    1 Corinthians 14:2 NKJV

Oftentimes, there can be a blockage within the one who is sick, hindering the healing process. The Helper can *reveal the mystery* as to what this blockage is.

Once, while ministering with a team in Guatemala, the missionary asked us to visit a woman who was paralyzed from the waist down. The doctors were puzzled as to the cause of this paralysis and were unable to do anything for her. We agreed to visit this woman, but first we spent time praying in the Spirit. It was at that time the mystery was revealed to us that this woman had unforgiveness in her heart. This all came about by spending time with the Revealer of Mysteries; our Helper.

Mark 11:25 makes it very clear that we must always forgive. This should be made clear to the person you are praying for, if the Holy Spirit has revealed to you they have *a spirit of unforgiveness*. Share these two Scriptures with them.

> *And whenever you stand praying, if you have any-thing against anyone, forgive him, that your Father in heaven may also forgive you your trespasses.*
> Mark 11:25 NKJV

> *For assuredly, I say to you, whoever says to this moun-tain, 'Be removed and be cast into the sea,' and does not doubt in his heart, but believes that those things he says will be done, he will have whatever he says.*
> Mark 11:23 NKJV

A mountain can certainly be a sickness or disease. When dealing with someone struggling with forgiveness, such as the case with this woman from Guatemala, it is important they understand that if they don't have faith to forgive *one* offense, they will not have faith to move a mountain. When praying for the sick, we want their faith connecting with ours, so dealing with unforgiveness is crucial.

Once we explained to this woman the destruction that comes from unforgiveness and the healing power that comes through forgiveness, she wept, acknowledging she was filled with anger and unforgiveness toward two people who had deeply hurt her. We were then able to lead her through the process of forgiveness.

Later that evening we had an evangelistic service in that small village and ten minutes before the service began, she walked in. Are you wondering what happened after we left her home and when she arrived at the service? Shortly after we left her home, she received her healing and then *walked* to the meeting place; set free of paralysis and no longer a slave to an offense holding her in bondage. All this took place through the *help* of the Holy Spirit. Forgiveness is God's medicine that heals the pain of an offense. Once the inner healing took place, the manifestation of the physical healing took place as well.

The Apostle Paul knew the importance of the supply of the Holy Spirit.

> *For I know that this will turn out for my deliverance through your prayer and the supply of the Spirit of Jesus Christ.*
> Philippians 1:19 NKJV

To abandon the help of the Holy Spirit is to abandon the supply of the Holy Spirit.

> *Draw near to God and He will draw near to you.*
> James 4:8 NKJV

We must draw close to the Revealer of Secrets and receive His supply. How glorious it is that we have this Heavenly supply to *guide us into all truth and reveal the hidden things*. This flows from intimacy with the Father.

The Natural Working with the Supernatural

To be fruitful in praying for the sick, it takes the natural working together with the *supernatural*. The natural part is laying hands on the sick with the prayer of faith and the supernatural is the Healer who does the healing. We are not the Healer, but vessels through which the healing power of the Holy Spirit flows.

Healing has been purchased for everyone. However, we must guard our hearts against discouragement when not everyone receives healing. We don't have all the answers, but the Lord will reveal to us what we need to know.

> *The secret things belong to the LORD our God, but those things which are revealed belong to us...*
> Deuteronomy 29:29 NKJV

Not everyone will receive salvation, although both salvation and healing have been purchased and made available for all.

> *For God so loved the world that He gave His only begotten Son, that whoever believes in Him should*

not perish but have everlasting life. For God did not send His Son into the world to condemn the world, but that the world through Him might be saved.

John 3:16-17 NKJV

The word *saved* mentioned in the Scripture above means to be rescued in time, to be healed and to be made whole.

Surely He has borne our griefs and carried our sorrows; Yet we esteemed Him stricken, smitten by God, and afflicted. But He was wounded for our transgressions, He was bruised for our iniquities; The chastisement for our peace was upon Him, And by His stripes we are healed.

Isaiah 53:4-5 NKJV

This Scripture covers the total man: *spirit, soul* and *body*. It is important to remember that regardless of what does or does not happen—stay with the Word. We do not have all the answers, but we move forward with what we do know and obey the *Great Commission (Mark 16:15-18)*.

Prayer and Fasting

In Matthew 17:18-24 we read the story of Jesus rebuking the demon and the child was cured. He then tells His disciples in verse 21 that this comes about through prayer and fasting.

What is the significance of fasting? For me, I find it increases my sensitivity to the leading of the Holy Spirit. It causes the ear of my spirit to become more sensitive to His Voice within. This is another way of drawing on the divine supply of the Spirit. We must always draw from within.

We can't just come from the golf course, so-to-speak, and then to the hospital room. We must spend time with the Holy Spirit in order to be sensitive to His guidance. He will give us a word in season or reveal the root of the problem that hinders the healing process.

The Scripture above, Isaiah 53:4-5, refers to the spirit, soul and body. Often, the healing of the soul must come before healing of the body; this was the case with the woman in Guatemala. The root of a sickness cannot be ignored. The assignment of the Holy Spirit is to reveal truth which opens the door for us to be a blessing to those who need prayer.

Make the decision to spend time with the Revealer of Secrets. It is the Lord's desire that when we pray, we bear much fruit which only comes through vital union with Him.

> *Finally, my brethren, be strong in the Lord and in the power of His might.*
>
> Ephesians 6:10

Chapter 2

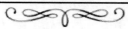

God's Will and His Ways

In preparing to pray for the sick, you must have it settled within YOUR heart that God wants everyone healed as much as He wants everyone saved.

There are many different beliefs, opinions, false teachings and lots of confusion about God's will and His ways. According to the Word, it is an unwise person who doesn't understand His will. He is not trying to hide this from us, but rather it is our responsibility to study His Word that we might come to know His will and ways. Always stay with the Word for it is His will.

> *Therefore do not be unwise, but understand what the will of the Lord is.*
>
> Ephesians 5:17

There are several reasons that cause a lack of knowledge. Someone once said, *"The success of the devil is determined by our lack of knowledge."* This is so true.

> *My people are destroyed for lack of knowledge.*
>
> Hosea 4:6 AMP

> *Study to shew thyself approved unto God, a workman that needeth not to be ashamed, rightly dividing the word of truth.*
>
> 2 Timothy 2:15 KJV

In this chapter, I will address questions that need to be answered, which will help in rightly dividing the Word of truth, regarding the will and the ways of God.

I can remember as a child, my mother always prayed regardless of the situation, *"Lord, if it be thy will."* Like so many, she did not know the will of God. The word *'if'* implies doubt and a lack of knowledge of His will.

1. Is it God's Will that Every Person Be Healed?

> *The Lord is not slack concerning His promise, as some count slackness, but is longsuffering toward us, not willing that any should perish but that all should come to repentance.*
>
> 2 Peter 3:9 NKJV

> *For God so loved the world that He gave His only*

14

begotten Son, that whoever believes in Him should not perish but have everlasting life. For God did not send His Son into the world to condemn the world, but that the world through Him might be saved.

John 3:16-17 NKJV

Will everyone recover and be healed? No. Will everyone be saved? No. Yet does God want everyone to be saved? Yes. Does God want everyone to be healed? Yes. Healing is a part of the Atonement *(Isaiah 53:4-5).*

Stay with the Word regardless of what does or does not happen to someone else, healed or not healed.

Some individuals will have their faith in your prayers only, and determine God's will by their results. Once you pray, if they are not healed, then they may judge what they see or feel as being God's will. They may conclude that healing is not God's will for them! They are walking by sight (the five senses) and not by faith.

2. Is Everything that Happens God's Will?

It's very tragic when a young person dies or when a parent is killed, leaving small children behind. So many times I've heard people say, *"It must have been God's will,"* or, *"Everything happens for a purpose."* This reveals a lack of knowledge regarding John 10:10, that the devil comes to steal, kill and destroy; not God. Stealing, killing and destroying is the devil's will and sole purpose. The devil is self-employed. God doesn't use the devil's assistance in getting His children into Heaven, nor does He need another angel in Heaven.

We see so many hate crimes, resulting in the killing of many innocent victims throughout the world. It is clearly stated in the Ten Commandments, *"Thou shalt not kill" (Exodus 20:13).*

The Scriptures also say that *thou shalt not commit adultery, steal nor covet,* yet we see this happening continually as well.

As previously mentioned in 2 Peter 3:9, *God is not willing that any should perish.* There are many who are rejecting the Lordship of Jesus Christ. Therefore, many shall not enter into Heaven, but rather, they shall enter the gates of hell and perish throughout all eternity.

Therefore, we cannot say that everything that happens is God's will.

> *For God so loved the world that He gave His only begotten Son, that whoever believes in Him should not perish but have everlasting life.*
> John 3:16 NKJV

3. Many Believe that God Can Do Anything

This is another wrong teaching or belief. It causes people to become angry at God when their loved one is not healed. They blame God for this.

God's love for mankind is unconditional, immeasurable and never ending. We could say His love for us is *off the charts,* Hallelujah! He wants everyone healed, however there are hindrances to healing, as well as causes for sickness and premature deaths.

> *Do not be overly wicked, nor be foolish: Why should you die before your time?*
>
> Ecclesiastes 7:17 NKJV

According to this Scripture, we see that it is possible to depart this earth prematurely. We are to fulfill God's plan and purpose for our lives. He *so* loves us, but has set limitations upon Himself by giving man a free will. A free will to love and obey Him, and to not be foolish or do things that are harmful to our bodies, causing sickness and in some cases premature death.

If God could do anything, He would make everyone get saved, attend church, read their Bible, tithe and love one another at all times. However, this is not His way. He gave every person a free will.

If He were in control of all that happened on the earth, there would be no stealing, no murder and no terrorist attacks. There would be no need for the Church, Evangelists or the Great Commission.

God originally gave dominion to Adam, who in turn gave it to Satan, thereby, allowing him to operate as the ruler of the kingdom of the air.

> *As for you, you were dead in your transgressions and sins, in which you used to live when you followed the ways of this world and of the ruler of the kingdom of the air, the spirit who is now at work in those who are disobedient.*
>
> Ephesians 2:1-2 NIV

Although God is sovereign, it is through prayer that we give God permission to intervene. Here is a powerful quote from *Dr. Lillian B. Yomans: *"God has tied Himself irrevocably to human cooperation in the execution of divine purposes. He has made man's faith a determining factor in the work of redemption."*

*Living by Faith by Lillian B. Yeomans

4. What About God's Timing?

For He says: "In an acceptable time I have heard you,

and in the day of salvation I have helped you." Behold, now is the accepted time; behold, now is the day of salvation.

2 Corinthians 6:2 NKJV

There is never a time when it's not the *time* to receive Jesus Christ as Savior, with the assurance of eternal life. The sin of mankind caused man to be separated from God throughout eternity. The love of God, which was powerfully demonstrated through the *death, burial and resurrection of Jesus*, made it possible for man to be restored back into fellowship with God *(John 3:16)*.

This truth is beautifully expressed in Isaiah 53:5, which clarifies that restoration with God is for the total man: spirit, soul and body. This is referred to as our Atonement.

But He was wounded for our transgressions, He was bruised for our iniquities; the chastisement for our peace was upon Him, and by His stripes we are healed.

Isaiah 53:5

The first section of this verse reveals salvation (restoration) for the spirit of man: *But He was wounded for our transgressions, He was bruised for our iniquities.* When we receive Jesus as our personal Savior, we are immediately translated from the kingdom of darkness into the Kingdom of His beloved Son Jesus, and we become a child of God.

*Who hath delivered us from the power of darkness,
and hath translated us into the kingdom of his dear
Son:*
Colossians 1:13 KJV

The middle section of Isaiah 53:5 refers to man's soulish realm: *the chastisement for our peace was upon Him.*
You will encounter people who live on a roller coaster of
emotions or who are codependent on negative memories
of their past. Calvary made it possible for the child of
God to be delivered from the enslavement of the past and
from the unexpected storms of life. Our soulish realm
can be restored.

*He makes me to lie down in green pastures; He leads
me beside the still waters. He restores my soul...*
Psalm 23:2-3a NKJV

*Peace I leave with you, My peace I give to you; not as
the world gives do I give to you. Let not your heart
be troubled, neither let it be afraid.*
John 14:27 NKJV

There is a peace that has been purchased for the child
of God which is not available to those who have yet to
receive Jesus as their personal Savior. This peace is available to the believer at the moment of receiving the free
gift of eternal life.

The last section of Isaiah 53:5 is speaking about man's physical body: *and by His stripes we are healed.* This is not referring to inner healing. Inner healing is covered in the restoration of man's soulish realm.

The word *and* beginning the last section of this verse is a conjunction. The purpose of the conjunction *and* is to join words, phrases, and clauses of equal value within a sentence. Therefore, since all three sections of Isaiah 53:5 are joined together, we can be confident that healing is also available to the believer at the moment of receiving the free gift of eternal life.

In addition to healing being available for the believer because it is part of our covenant with God, He will heal the unbeliever through His grace, drawing them to surrender their life to Jesus.

> *Or do you despise the riches of His goodness, forbearance, and longsuffering, not knowing that the goodness of God leads you to repentance?*
> Romans 2:4 NKJV

During one of my healing seminars in Slovakia, an unsaved man was healed of an advanced stage of cancer. A woman from the church invited her cousin Stanley to attend. He made it very clear to her that he was not interested in any such seminar. Through her persistence, however, he finally agreed to come the last night.

At this time I knew nothing about Stanley. At the end of my teaching, I gave an invitation for salvation. Several people responded. I then proceeded to pray for the sick. A number of people came forward, including Stanley. As I stood in front of him, I knew by the Spirit of the Lord that he was not saved, so I asked if he had ever given his life to the Lord. He replied, *"No, I have not."* I asked, *"Would you like to do that tonight?"*

"No, I would not." He replied without any hesitation. *"I don't want any of that stuff."* Not the response I was expecting, but I stayed neutral and continued to speak.

"So, what exactly do you want?" I asked him. *"I just want your God to heal me and take away all this pain, but I don't want any of that other stuff."* he repeated.

I began to tell him how much my God loved him and that I would pray for his healing. The next day I was scheduled to fly to the Czech Republic, but before leaving I called the Pastor and asked if he could pick me up early because I wanted to see Stanley. I *so* wanted him to receive salvation. The Pastor said he would come early, but just before I called, the woman from the church called the Pastor with a great report. Stanley was completely free of pain and believed God had healed him.

Well, Stanley was very surprised that I came to his home. I asked, *"Do you remember I told you my God loves you?"* With a peaceful countenance and gentle smile, he replied, *"Yes, I remember, but now I know."* He then gave his heart to the Lord. Truly this is an example of the goodness of the Lord drawing men to repentance. Today is always the day to receive healing as much as it is to receive eternal life because of God's love for all humanity.

> *For He says: "In an acceptable time I have heard you, and in the day of salvation I have helped you." Behold, now is the accepted time; behold, now is the day of salvation.*
>
> 2 Corinthians 6:2 NKJV

Praying with Confidence

Let us not be unwise, but know the will of the Lord. Once you have this settled in your heart, it makes it easier to pray with confidence, boldness and authority as God's Ambassador. Stay with the Word and the will of God regardless of what does or does not happen.

Chapter 3

Those Needing Prayer

Over the years I have prayed for people from different walks of life and religious backgrounds. Some had absolutely no knowledge of healing or didn't even think that healing was for today. Others had wrong information, such as thinking God was wanting to teach them something through sickness. Then there were others who didn't believe they were worthy to receive healing because of their past lifestyle.

As previously mentioned, the Lord wants everyone to be healed as much as He wants everyone to be saved. However, there are different reasons why healing does not always happen. It's important that we understand some of these factors. We don't have all the answers, but we need to look at what we do know.

Let's look at the different reasons individuals, who are in need of healing, haven't received their healing. This is critical for us to know in order to be as fruitful as the Lord has equipped us to be.

I've categorized these individuals by groups and listed relevant Scriptures. Of course, these are not the only Scriptures you can use, simply a few suggestions, and the ones I use most often.

FIRST GROUP:
Those Having No Knowledge of Healing

Unfortunately there are believers as well as non-believers who actually have no knowledge of God's will to heal. We can understand why the Word says according to Hosea 4:6 AMP, *"My people are destroyed for lack of knowledge."* Therefore, the door is open for the devil to steal, kill and destroy *(John 10:10b)*.

It's possible that some of the people you will encounter may never have heard about the Lord, His love for them, or may have never even been inside a church.

Our first step is to show them what the Word of God says regarding His love and His desire to heal, and to let them know His Word is His will.

In my opinion, John 3:16-17 is always a good place to start, with emphasis on verse 17.

For God so loved the world that He gave His only begotten Son, that whoever believes in Him should not perish but have everlasting life. For God did not send His Son into the world to condemn the world, but that the world through Him might be saved.
John 3:16-17 NKJV

It's also very beneficial to point out that the word *saved* includes healing. He wants to be their Healer and Savior.

The following are excellent Scriptures to share.

- Isaiah 53:4-5   Healed by His stripes
- I Peter 2:24   Healed by His stripes
- Matthew 4:23   Jesus healed all
- Hebrews 13:8   Jesus Christ is the same
- Romans 3:23, 6:23, 10:9-10   Path to salvation

After sharing the above Scriptures, encourage them to pray the prayer of the Apostle Paul in Ephesians 1:16-23, which helps to increase their knowledge of God's will for them. Show them how to personalize the Word as they read it, for example:

That the God of our Lord Jesus Christ, the Father of glory, may give to (me) the spirit of wisdom and revelation [that gives you a deep and personal and

intimate insight] in the knowledge of Him...
Ephesians 1:17 AMP

Regarding salvation, don't push it if they're not ready. I have experienced that healing can often be the dinner bell to salvation. I have prayed for people who received healing, but were not saved. In the previous chapter I mentioned Stanley who was very adamant about not wanting to be saved, but did want to be free of pain and sickness. Such individuals the Lord will still heal, and after experiencing His love and goodness, their hearts will become open to receive Him as their Savior, and not just their Healer. The goodness of the Lord brings men to repentance *(Romans 2:4)*.

SECOND GROUP:
Those Who Have Received
Wrong Knowledge of Healing

Wrong information such as:

- God is trying to teach them something through their sickness.
- They are not worthy to receive His love and healing.
- Healing is not for everyone.

The Scriptures tell us that the truth of the Gospel will set us free *(John 8:32)*. After sharing the following Scriptures with them, encourage them to pray the prayer of the Apostle Paul in Ephesians 1:16-23, which will help to increase their knowledge of God's will for them personally. Again, show them to personalize the Word as mentioned in the First Group.

The following are excellent Scriptures to share.

- 2 Timothy 3:16   God teaches us through His Word
- Romans 8:35-36   Nothing can separate us from His love
- John 3:16   Healing is for everyone
- Isaiah 53:4-5   Healing by His stripes
- Matthew 4:23   Jesus healed all
- Hebrews 13:8   Jesus Christ is the same forever

THIRD GROUP:
Those Having Correct Knowledge, but Fail to Be a Doer of the Word

This group simply needs a little encouragement, support and direction. Sometimes accountability with a prayer partner or the prayer of agreement will help. They may also need direction in taking their spiritual authority, as well as further teaching on how to take God's Word as medicine to their flesh *(Proverbs 4:22)*.

Encourage them to surround themselves with others who believe in healing and who will stand with them and help them through the tough days. If they are not able to do this, encourage them not to share their situation with unsaved family members, but only with those who will help strengthen and encourage them in their faith.

The following are excellent Scriptures to share.

- 2 Timothy 2:15 We are to study the Word
- James 1:22 Be a doer of the Word
- Matthew 18:18-20 Prayer of Agreement
- Luke 10:19 Authority of the believer
- Proverbs 4:20-22 God's Word is medicine

You may also encounter Christians who are just spiritually lazy and need to spend more time in the Word and be a doer of it. I've even had people acknowledge to me that they are lazy, but don't seem to want to change. For this individual, I encourage them to pray the prayers of the Apostle Paul in Ephesians 1:16-23 and 3:14-21 for spiritual enlightenment and inner strength.

Other than this, there's not much more you can do for this person. Like the old saying goes, *"You can lead a horse to the water, but you can't make him drink."*

FOURTH GROUP:
Those Who Are Angry With God

We have all suffered deep sorrows and painful disappointments in life. When someone loses a loved one and doesn't understand the will and ways of God, they can become angry with Him. They can feel betrayed and abandoned, losing all trust in the Lord; these cannot even begin to believe for their own healing.

Encourage them that God's love for them will never end nor fail, and that He cares deeply about their pain and suffering. Explain that to be angry and turn their back on Him, is to turn away from the very One who can help and heal their pain.

It's helpful if we can get them to express their feelings to God. Share that as we pour out our hearts to God, even in anger, He will begin to heal their pain. This in itself can bring deliverance and freedom, enabling us to take them to a new and closer walk with the Lord.

The following are excellent Scriptures to share.

- Psalm 34:18-19   God heals the broken-hearted
- Psalm 46:1-2   He is a present help

31

- Psalm 73:26   He is the strength of our hearts
- Hebrews 13:5b   He will never leave us
- Jeremiah 16:19   Lord is my strength
- John 10:10   The thief comes to kill and destroy

FIFTH GROUP:
Those Who Call for the Elders of the Church

Is anyone among you sick? Let him call for the elders of the church, and let them pray over him, anointing him with oil in the name of the Lord.

> *And the prayer of faith will save the sick, and the Lord will raise him up.*
>
> James 5:15a NKJV

Let's take a close look at these two verses.

- **First:** *The One Who is Sick.*

The word *sick* implies someone who is extremely ill or an invalid and unable to come to church. These are those suffering with more than a minor ailment or a headache, but rather physically frail, feeble perhaps even terminally ill and confined to their home. This precious person who is loved by God has the biblical right to call *with urgency* for the elders of the church to come.

32

▪ **Second:** *The Elders of the Church.*

This person should be an ordained minister or hold an official position in the church.

Often a family member or friend wants you to come to the hospital or home to pray for their loved one or friend. It's important to explain the Scripture in James 5:14 to the family member, letting them know it's important that the one needing prayer, request for an elder of the church to come. That doesn't mean the sick person has to make the phone call, but asking the family member to do it on their behalf.

However, if the one sick is not making this request, we don't want the family to think we're not willing to pray. This is why you must be sensitive to the leading of the Holy Spirit as to the best approach for the situation.

Once you have this opportunity there is the possibility of leading the person to Christ if they are not saved. You might discover the person is angry with God or has very little knowledge of His love and His desire to heal. In either of these cases, you can refer to the suggestions mentioned in one of the previous groups.

▪ **Third:** *Anointing With Oil in the Name of Jesus.*

Although the Bible refers to olive oil, if this is not available, another type of oil can be used. Oil in itself has no healing power, but implies the presence of the Holy Spirit with the power to heal. As the oil is applied with prayer, this is the moment the sick person is to release their faith joined with yours, bringing healing and wholeness to their body.

As the elders pray in the Name of Jesus, it represents full authority as Christ's Ambassadors. As diplomatic agents of the highest rank we are authorized to speak on behalf of Christ with the Voice of Heaven.

▪ Fourth: *The Lord Shall Raise Him Up.*

Again, this implies one who is suffering from more than a minor ailment, but critically ill even to the point of death. The prayer of faith shall raise him up. This is the powerful and beautiful example of the natural working together with the supernatural as mentioned in Chapter 1.

Learn to flow with the dynamic power within you. What an awesome privilege and joy to see someone restored back to health. It takes our faith and obedience as His Ambassadors fulling the Great Commission. To God be all the glory!

We must pray for the sick with the same compassion that Jesus had when He prayed for the sick. Let it be that heart-felt prayer of the righteous man able to bear much fruit.

... the earnest (heartfelt, continued) prayer of a

righteous man makes tremendous power available [dynamic in its working].

James 5:16b AMPC

SIXTH GROUP:
Those Who Ask for Prayer, but Truthfully Don't Want to Be Healed

You're probably thinking…WHAT? That was my first reaction when I heard the Holy Spirit whisper that to me regarding someone I had been praying for over a long period of time. In addition to the church praying, friends and every guest minister, I finally asked the Lord what the delay was and that's when I heard those words, *"She didn't want to be healed."*

Immediately I knew why. A few days later when I met with this person, I asked; *"Do you really want to be healed?"* *"Of course."* was her reply. I proceeded to ask, *"If you are healed are you aware of the fact you will no longer qualify for disability?"* She then softly replied as she hung her head, *"Yes, I know that."* I then asked, *"Are you willing to give up that monthly disability check?"* Her answer, *"NO."*

She then acknowledged that she really didn't want to be healed, but wanted people to think that she did. She always confessed healing Scriptures and said all the right things in the presence of others, but none of it was sincere.

With a loving attitude, I told her that it was her prerogative to not want to be healed. I encouraged her however, not to get in the prayer line any longer and play games with God or people's emotions. This causes confusion to the Body of Christ when they don't see people being healed who are repeatedly being prayed for and continually confessing healing Scriptures.

In situations like this, I have tried to encourage the individual that the same God who heals is also the same God who supplies all our needs. But you often find the person doesn't want to get a job and have to work. They prefer to accept the sickness or disease, if they can tolerate it, and receive a disability check rather than having to work.

This also applies to an insecure person who doesn't want healing because they don't want to lose the attention they are getting. The Scriptures that pertain to who they are in Christ would also be helpful for this individual.

The following are excellent Scriptures to share.

- Philippians 4:19 KJV   God supplies our needs
- Ephesians 1:17 AMP   Spiritual enlightenment
- Ephesians 3:16-21 AMP   Inner strength

In each of these situations or groups, remember salvation is the greatest miracle of all. Always introduce Jesus to the one who has no knowledge or wrong knowledge, but never be forceful. If they're not ready, just plant the seed. The Scriptures I have shared are of course not the only ones for you to use, this is just a guideline. You may even find that what you use for one group will also be appropriate for another group. There will be some of these beautiful people that God loves and wants healed, who may not even have a Bible or know how to look up specific Scriptures. It's vitally important to help them in this journey of getting to know more about the Lord through His Word.

The Holy Spirit is Our Helper

Never bypass the help of the Holy Spirit. I can't encourage you enough on the *importance* of being very sensitive to the Spirit of the Lord. He is your Guide and Helper. He will guide you into the truth of what to do and to say. Therefore, be built up in prayer and sensitive to the Spirit. I have encountered numerous situations where the Helper revealed the root of the problem. Until this is dealt with, physical healing can be hindered.

You will recall the story mentioned on pages 7 through 9 regarding the women in Guatemala who was paralyzed. As we began to pray for her healing, the Holy Spirit gave an inward witness to one of the team members that there was a deeper issue involved.

She shared with us regarding the abuse from her husband, who was no longer living. While she was speaking, the anger that was still residing in her heart began to flare up. I then knew she needed to know the power of forgiveness. I explained that forgiveness never means the offense is okay, but that forgiveness is God's way of healing the pain of the offense. Regardless of whether the offender is living or not, forgiveness is for her benefit, not his. If there is no faith to forgive one offense, there will never be enough faith to remove a mountain of sickness or disease, nor will God forgive our offenses *(Mark 11:23-26).*

She was very open to this and wanted to be healed from what her husband had done. After she prayed and forgave him, we then prayed for her healing.

Once the root of the problem was dealt with, the physical healing could, and did take place. The root of the problem was revealed by the Holy Spirit.

Eye has not seen, nor ear heard, nor have entered into the heart of man the things which God has prepared for those who love Him. But God has revealed them to us through His Spirit. For the Spirit searches all things, yes, the deep things of God.
                    1 Corinthians 2:9-10 NKJV

For he who speaks in a tongue does not speak to men,

but to God, for no one understands him; however, in the spirit he speaks mysteries.

1 Corinthians 14:2 NKJV

It is so vital that we rely on the Holy Spirit because He is the Revealer of Secrets. Some things are a mystery to us, but never to our Helper.

Truly your God is the God of gods, the Lord of kings, and a revealer of secrets, since you could reveal this secret.

Daniel 2:47 NKJV

We must always keep ourselves built up, staying sensitive to our Helper, and staying in the love of God.

But you, beloved, building yourselves up on your most holy faith, praying in the Holy Spirit, keep yourselves in the love of God, looking for the mercy of our Lord Jesus Christ unto eternal life.

Jude 20-21 NKJV

But you have an anointing from the Holy One [you have been set apart, specially gifted and prepared by the Holy Spirit], and all of you know [the truth because He teaches us, illuminates our minds, and guards us from error].

I John 2:20 AMP

When praying for the sick, don't bypass the ministry of the Holy Spirit because you may have only one opportunity to pray with them. By praying in our Heavenly language, we increase our sensitivity to His leading and His direction. Many times He reveals the answer to us through an inward knowing or a still small voice.

As we pray in the Holy Spirit, we keep our spirit in tune with His Spirit.

Chapter 4

Why Some Don't Receive Healing

There are different reasons why healing does not always happen. We know that unforgiveness can definitely hinder healing. However, in this chapter, I am addressing other factors that may hinder them from *receiving* their healing. Factors that can cause confusion and doubt in the hearts of loved ones and friends regarding the truth of faith and healing.

> *The secret things belong to the LORD our God, but the things revealed belong to us and to our children forever...*
>
> Deuteronomy 29:29 NIV

From this Scripture we see that there are secrets that belong to the Lord. The word *secret* means: that which has been set apart from the knowledge of others.

This verse continues to state that some things are revealed

and not kept secret. It's important that we obtain insight into the things that are revealed. We don't have all the answers, but we need to look at what we do know. Jesus is the Healer and wants everyone healed.

Here's a question that I believe is important to address and that I have been asked so many times. I'm sure you've heard it as well. *"Why did so-and-so die? I know they were in faith."*

I would like to share from one of my healing miracles (See page 75) and see it from the view point as if I *DID NOT* receive a miracle, and consequently died.

When I was 28 years old, I was miraculously healed of cancer. While in the hospital and within minutes of being prepped for surgery, I had a beautiful encounter with the Lord. I actually heard what seemed to be an audible voice which I heard three times.

First: *"Your time is up. Under your present condition you are destined to die."*

After a short pause, I then heard, *"Your life has been removed from the hands of mankind: your condition is now beyond the help of the medical profession."*

Another short pause, I heard the words from the *Gospel*

of John: "I am the way, the Truth and the Life. Through Me you can change your destiny."

When I heard those Words, which I had read so many times from the Bible, I knew I was truly hearing from the Lord. I responded immediately and received a miracle. Let's imagine however, what would have happened had I not responded as I did and consequently died?

Remember the Words I first heard, *"Your time is up. Under your present condition you are destined to die."*

Had I died, it would have brought confusion to my family and friends causing them to question, *"Why did God let Marilyn die?"* or, *"Why didn't God heal Marilyn?"* Or they could have thought, *"It must have been her time."* All of these questions and comments are understandable, coming from people who do not have a solid Biblical foundation.

I know had I not responded as I did, my private and intimate time with the Lord would have remained a secret. No one would have known what He said to me. No one would have known that I had a glorious encounter with my Heavenly Father, giving me the opportunity to receive a healing miracle.

When my mother was transitioning from this life to the next, my brothers and I visited her every day at the hospital. As the end was drawing close, we each went into her room privately to have a special loving good-bye. To this day, I don't know what my brothers said to her nor do they know what I said to her. It has remained a secret. It was our own private time with our mother.

When I was in the hospital awaiting surgery, the Lord revealed His love and healing power to me privately. Again, had I not responded as I did, my private time with the Lord would have remained a secret forever. However, it is not a secret for I have shared my testimony to the nations.

God is not a respecter of persons. I believe that He has a private time with all His children. Some respond differently than others. Some fail to receive their healing and die, leaving loved ones questioning God. Some get angry with God and others question if healing is even real.

Let me emphasize, it's always okay to ask God a question, but it is not okay to question God. By this I mean, we are not to question or wonder if healing is for today or for everyone. This is important for us to understand that when ministering to others who don't understand why their loved one didn't receive healing, since truly believing their loved one was in faith.

Therefore, encourage those desiring to ask God a question, it's perfectly alright to do so. As they continue to attend church and read the Bible, that's when God will answer. But if they remain angry with God and refuse to stay in fellowship with the Lord, the answer will not be heard.

Why Some Respond as They Do

The stories I am about to share are true, but I have changed the names. Perhaps these stories will help to answer the question, *"Why did my loved one die? I know he/she was in faith."*

Became Weary

Clyde knew the power of healing, but had grown tired in his fight of faith and gave up. He became weary and simply wanted to go home *(I Timothy 6:12)*.

> *Let us not become weary in doing good, for at the proper time we will reap a harvest if we do not give up.*
> Galatians 6:9 NIV

The pain experienced during a horrible and destructive disease can sometimes be overwhelming. Clyde made the decision to depart and be with Christ, which we know is far better, we must not judge his faith.

Repeatedly, I see so many that do get weary and give up. The fight of faith is not always an easy fight, but the Word encourages us to not grow weary and to not give up. We must not judge anyone who gives up and desires to go home to be with the Lord. Yes, they will be missed, but we must never judge. When praying for the sick, we need to pray for their inner strength so they won't get weary and give up.

I pray that out of His glorious riches He may strengthen you with power through his Spirit in your inner being.

Ephesians 3:16 NIV

Several years ago, I was on my death bed with Malaria. This Ephesians' prayer was the one prayer I requested. I knew I had to stay strong inwardly, so I would not give up, and consequently not receive my healing.

Stopped Fighting

Sylvia, a very close friend, and I attended the same church which was very strong in teaching on faith and healing. Sylvia was undergoing chemotherapy and was winning the battle of cancer.

Oftentimes, receiving chemotherapy has negative side effects causing people to become ill for several days after each treatment. So it was with Sylvia. One day I went to her home to help her in any way that I could. Her teenage daughter was there and when Sylvia asked her daughter to do something, her daughter gave a huge sigh and spoke harshly, letting her mother know she was getting tired of this and wanted to go out with her friends.

It upset me to see her response to her mother's need. As politely as I could, I said, *"I know this is your mother, but she is also my friend and I'm asking you not to speak like that to my friend. Why don't you just go and be with your friends and I'll take care of my friend today?"* And so it was.

After several of Sylvia's treatments she had been encouraged by the doctor that the chemo seemed to be working and she was on her way to recovery. She still had a number of treatments ahead of her, but was doing very well. After a few months, she was getting close to the end of her treatments.

During one of these latter treatments, I went to be with her at the hospital. As soon as I entered her room, I knew something was wrong, I could sense it in the spirit. With great concern I asked her, *"What's happened Sylvia? I can tell something's wrong – what is it? Tell me, let me help."* I didn't like what I was sensing.

She then told me her adult son had come to see her earlier that day. He informed Sylvia that he was taking care of everything and she didn't have to be concerned about anything because he had given some of her furniture away and had already put her house on the market. With tears in her eyes, she said, *"I was planning on having a complete recovery, but it seems that my family is tired of me and preparing for me to die, so I've decided to go to Heaven and be with the Lord."* This broke my heart and there was nothing I could do or say to heal her disappointment with how her family was responding to her illness.

Sylvia was feeling very unloved and sensing she had become a burden to her family. It is heart-wrenching to see those you care so much about who are fighting with every breath they breathe to live and not die, and then, to sense that they are no longer loved or wanted.

In situations like this, it is understandable why they would make the decision to depart and be with Jesus, the One whose love never ends. It was only a few days later that Sylvia passed on to Heaven.

At that point many in the church questioned, *"Why did Sylvia die? I know she was in faith."*

Yes, she was in faith, but stopped fighting. Not everyone knew the whole story. We don't always see the whole picture, therefore confusion sets in. People can begin to doubt whether healing or faith really works. Faith always works and this is why it's so important we stay with the Word regardless if someone does or does not receive healing, again, we don't know the whole story. *"The secret things belong to the Lord,"* *(Deuteronomy 29:29).*

Feeling Unloved

Almost the identical thing happened to my friend Susie. She too was strong in faith and undergoing chemotherapy. One Friday evening after dinner I went to visit her. Her teenagers were about to leave the house for the evening to be with their friends. In Susie's frail voice she whispered for them to come back to say good night. With a huge sigh they said, *"Mom, we're in a hurry, we don't have time now"* and rushed out. The look on her face was heart-breaking. I could hardly hold back the tears myself. She then asked her husband to help her to the bathroom, for which she regularly needed his assistance. Unfortunately, he also responded with a huge sigh and said, *"Again?"*

It was a no-brainer to sense she was feeling very unloved and that she had become a huge burden to her family. I believe it was at that moment she made the decision, as did my friend Sylvia, to stop fighting the good fight of faith and depart to be with the Lord. A couple of days later Susie was taken to the hospital, and then she also went home to Heaven. Again, here was the question by her family and friends: *"Why did she die? I know she was in faith."* Remember, not everyone knows the whole story nor do even the family members realize what they are doing.

Lack of Knowledge

This story is about a good friend. She attended a church that was not strong in their beliefs about healing or that God wanted everyone to be healed. Carol was a faithful member of this church and accepted their beliefs. She became sick with cancer and was undergoing chemotherapy, however she was not improving, but rather growing worse.

Since I was often on the road traveling for ministry, I would receive emails from Carol's friends telling me they were encouraged to see that she was strong in faith and believing for healing. I found this to be a little questionable knowing what she had been taught regarding healing, but I was hopeful that it was true. Her friends said she had been asking for me to come and visit when I returned home.

Carol had a loving husband and a teenage son, and every day one, if not more, of Carol's friends were at the house helping not only Carol, but also doing what they could for her husband and son. They were all working together. There was never a day that anyone felt burdened, and at no time did Carol ever feel unloved or that she was a burden to anyone.

When I returned home I went to see her. At this point she was no longer undergoing chemo. The doctors said there was nothing else they could do for her. Yet her friends were still so encouraged with Carol's faith. I went to visit her and asked graciously if I could be alone with her. One friend took great offense to this, which I knew she would, and that was why I made this request as humbly as I could. It was important that I be alone with Carol, knowing that I would be able to locate her faith when it was just the two of us.

Her friends were right, she was in great faith. They also saw the countenance upon her face reflecting the peace of God. But it was not great faith for healing that she had, rather, great faith that if she died, she would go to Heaven. Carol was only *in hope* to be healed. Because of the teaching she had, she was convinced that healing was not for everyone. At this stage there was no opening in her understanding that God wants everyone to be healed as much as He wants everyone saved.

Carol knew the right words to say in the presence of her friends and therefore, they understood her faith to be that Jesus was going to heal her. A couple weeks after I had been to see her, hospice had been scheduled for Carol as well as to prepare the family and friends.

After she passed away, there was that same question. *"Why did she die? I know she was in faith."* At the funeral, the pastor shared that healing is not for everyone. He said that God chooses whom He wants to heal even though He loves everyone.

What Carol's friends saw was God's grace, but they mistook that as faith to be healed. Perhaps you've noticed that when an immediate family is grieving the loss of a loved one, they seem to have it all together when preparing for, and during the funeral. However, it's really God's grace upon that family, and not their faith. You often hear people say, *"I don't know if I would have that much faith if I were going through all that."* I'm not putting down faith, but that is not what they are seeing; once again it's God's grace. That's why weeks after a funeral, the grieving family needs a lot of support from friends and comfort from the Holy Spirit. It is because now grace has lifted. It wasn't that they lost faith, but rather they were under God's umbrella of grace. We must be careful not to mistake faith for grace and then question healing when it doesn't happen.

I also want to point out how much love Carol sensed at all times, and that she had never become a burden to anyone. It's very sad that she had wrong teaching regarding God's will to heal *all (Hosea 4:6).*

Love Conquers

Let me share just one more story about someone I didn't know, but their Pastor shared this with me. This dear woman had *NOT* been taught much about faith or healing. She had been diagnosed with a terminal illness, but it would be a painful and slow process which would cause her to suffer over a long period of time. Repeatedly she told her husband and teenage son to not worry about her. She believed in God and knew that when she died, she would go to Heaven and be free of all pain.

This disease had taken its toll and death was at the door. The doctor permitted her to return home and spend her last day with her family. Her loving husband and son were at her bedside, and with a weak and frail voice, she once again told them not to worry about her. She knew she would be with the Lord, possibly, before the day was over.

Her son had heard these words numerous times before, but this time he broke down in tears crying out to her, *"Mom, I'm not worried about you, I'm worried about me! I need you!"* He then ran out of her room crying profusely.

At that moment with great determination, in a very weak voice Carol whixpered, *"God I can't die; my son needs me."* Suddenly a miracle happened. It was not an instant healing, but instead of dying that night, over a period of time she had a complete recovery.

What a beautiful story. She was motivated by *LOVE* to *LIVE*. There was never a time when she felt unloved or that she had become a burden to her family. What a powerful testimony.

Caregiver

If you have the opportunity to speak to a caregiver, let them know there is no condemnation in taking a break; it's a must. They need a break, even if they have to hire someone one day a week, or if possible, call the church to see if there is help available. When they get tired and exhausted, those feelings are passed on to the one who is sick and can have devastating results. It's not always easy taking care of someone, but we all need to be Jesus with *skin* on Him. Care with joy, love, physical and emotional strength, and a heart of compassion.

Trapped

Here are three Scriptures that are vital in understanding why some don't receive.

> *You have been trapped by what you said, ensnared by the words of your mouth.*
> Proverbs 6:2 NIV

It's easy to speak life-filled words on Sunday after hearing a powerful faith-filled message, but when the symptoms flare up on Monday, a trap can be set which will hinder the individual's healing. That's what the Bible warns us about. Speaking death-filled words instead of life-filled words will always set a trap.

Death and life are in the power of the tongue, And those who love it will eat its fruit.

Proverbs 18:27 NKJV

Death is not in the power of cancer or any other life threatening disease. Death is in the power of the tongue.

Words such as; *"Oh my back is killing me, my allergies are driving me crazy, I'm catching the flu, the doctor said... my condition is terminal, hopeless, I have three months to live."* These words are words of death and defeat. Instead, words of truth and life must be spoken, believed and acted upon.

Jesus said the truth shall set you free.

And you shall know the truth, and the truth shall make you free.

John 8:32 NKJV

When praying for the sick, remind them that God's Word is medicine. As they speak words of truth, they are applying God's medicine which has the power to heal.

My son, give attention to my words, Incline your ear to my sayings. Do not let them depart from your eyes; Keep them in the midst of your heart; For they are life to those who find them, and health

(medicine) to all their flesh.
Proverbs 4:20-22 NKJV

Cannot be Reversed

I want to close this chapter with one more reason why some don't receive healing.

There are individuals who have repeatedly spoken death-filled words over their life for long periods of time, even years, which has put a spiritual law into motion that can no longer be reversed. When words of death and defeat are spoken, that is what shall be; this is a spiritual law.

For assuredly, I say to you, whoever says to this mountain, 'Be removed and be cast into the sea,' and does not doubt in his heart, but believes that those things he says will be done, he will have whatever he says.
Mark 11:23 NKJV

I have heard several situations where the Lord revealed to the one who was praying for the sick, that the one sick had put an irreversible spiritual law of death into motion. Therefore, all the prayers for healing will be of no avail.

There are people who have confessed for years, that they would die before they reached a certain age, and it all came to pass. This was something they truly believed would happen.

Once again, a spiritual law that has been set in motion cannot be reversed and such individuals will not receive healing. This is an important truth to know when wondering why some don't receive. This is sad and very disappointing, but true for the Word of the Lord has spoken it.

Why Some Die When They Are in Faith

Prayerfully, I have answered questions that you might have had when confronting people who are angry with God, and have questions: *"Why did she/he die? I know she/he was in faith."* Perhaps this has given you some insights that you can share with those who have lost a loved one, or who may be confused and even angry with God. It might be good to share the Scripture in Deuteronomy 29:29 as the Lord leads. *The secret things belong to the Lord.*

Let the Holy Spirit guide you.

Chapter 5

Locating Faith

Jesus was able to locate people's faith. In the following Scriptures we see the different levels of faith.

▶ **No Faith:** Jesus refers in Mark 4:40 KJV to people having no faith. *"Why are you so fearful? How is it that you have no faith?"* We know that every person has been given a measure of faith (Romans 12:3), but Jesus is referring to those who never use their faith. Therefore, He says to them, that they have *no faith.* As they continued being with Jesus, He taught them further.

When we are praying with someone, never tell them they have no faith. Simply show them what the Word says and encourage them to trust in the Lord.

▶ **Little Faith:** In Matthew 8:26 KJV Jesus says, *"Why are you fearful, O you of little faith?"* Little faith is undeveloped faith. The more we use our faith, the more it is developed. Jesus saw that they were not developing their faith.

▶ **Weak Faith versus Strong Faith:** In the *Book of Romans* we read about the Father of Faith, Abraham.

And being not weak in faith, he considered not his own body now dead, when he was about an hundred years old, neither yet the deadness of Sarah's womb: He staggered not at the promise of God through unbelief; but was strong in faith...
Romans 4:19-20 KJV

Weak faith is faith divided between belief and unbelief, sometimes thinking God will help, and other times giving up all hope. This is called weak faith or one who is double minded.

If any of you lack wisdom, let him ask of God, that giveth to all men liberally, and upbraideth not; and it shall be given him. But let him ask in faith, nothing wavering. For he that wavereth is like a wave of the sea driven with the wind and tossed. For let not that man think that he shall receive any thing of the Lord. A double minded man is unstable in all his ways.
James 1:5-8 KJV

It is very clear here that one with weak faith is double

minded and receives nothing from the Lord. His prayers go unanswered and his needs unmet.

▶ **Great Faith:** In the *Gospel of Luke,* Jesus refers to the Centurion as one having great faith.

> *I tell you, I have not found such great faith even in Israel.*
>
> Luke 7:9 NKJV

I find this to be encouraging regarding great faith. If you are fully persuaded that when you die you will be with the Lord, this is great faith. Therefore, should you find yourself in a place of needing healing, use the great faith you have for salvation and make it work for you regarding your healing. This is something you can share with those you are praying with who have no hope for healing, yet great faith for salvation. As mentioned in the previous chapter, my friend had great faith believing she would go to Heaven if she was not healed. Encourage them to be fully persuaded that healing is for now while on this earth, the same as salvation is for when departing this earthly life.

▶ **Growing Faith:** This Scripture is encouraging to all of us and refers to growing faith.

> *We are bound to thank God always for you, brethren,*

as it is fitting, because your faith grows exceedingly, and the love of every one of you all abounds toward each other.

2 Thessalonians 1:3 NKJV

Renewing our minds *daily* and applying the Word *daily* causes our faith to grow *daily*.

▶ **Unfailing Faith:** When Jesus spoke to Peter, He said, *"I have prayed for thee, that thy faith fail not."*
(Luke 22:30-32 KJV)

As we continue to dwell in the secret place of the Most High God and stay with what the Word says, we guard our faith from failing.

The Voice of Faith

When praying for the sick [as with the story we read about Carol] learn to listen, and with the help of the Holy Spirit you will be able to locate their level of faith. Listening helps to give insight as to their knowledge of healing and their impression of God. Meet them where they are and then take them to the next level. Unfortunately with Carol, her heart was not open. But never tell someone they have no faith. It will destroy all of their hope. Remember that faith gives life to what we hope for.

Now faith is confidence in what we hope for and assurance about what we do not see.
Hebrews 11:1 NIV

Faith brings their hopes into reality, so we don't want to ever destroy someone's hope. Many of the people you pray for will be in hope of being healed. Meet them where they are and find a place of agreement by asking, *"What would you like me to pray?"*

Faith has a voice, so learn to listen. Let them talk, but don't let them drag out the problem. It won't take long to locate where they are spiritually. Don't try to force them to your level.

And since we have the same spirit of faith, according to what is written, "I believed and therefore I spoke," we also believe and therefore speak."
2 Corinthians 4:13 NKJV

Let me take you back several years when I was preaching to a group of Muslims in Indonesia. They saw themselves as Christians only because they were not practicing the Muslim religion. Remembering how important it is to meet people where they are and take them to the next level, I told them I was happy to hear that they were Christians. If I were to tell them they were not Christians, it's possible they would have all gotten up and walked out. So with great excitement in my voice, I told them that since they were Christians they could now have a personal relationship with Jesus Christ. They were pleasantly surprised to learn of this *Good News of the Gospel.* At that point, I began to preach on salvation and afterwards they all gave their lives to Christ. But once again, I had to meet them on their level before I was able to take them higher.

Last of all, be careful not to mistake God's loving grace for faith. God's grace can quickly shift into gear when the human body reaches its breaking point and that person seeks Heaven's release. This will also help to keep you anchored in your walk of faith and assurance that God wants everyone to be healed.

Chapter 6

Praying in a Hospital Setting

Some hospitals have very strict visiting hours. Upon arriving at the appropriate floor of the patient's room, even though it might be during visiting hours, check in at the nurse's station to make sure it is convenient. This is showing courtesy and respect for the privacy of the patient. They are there because of illness or an injury and are being treated at all hours of the day. Always show respect to the hospital staff and don't touch any equipment regardless of your knowledge in the medical field.

You will encounter different situations in which you will be praying, whether for an adult or a child. Regardless of who it is, remember you may only have one opportunity, so listen to the Voice of the Holy Spirit.

As mentioned previously, it's important to be sure that this individual wants you to visit them. Again, you may only have one opportunity to pray for them. As you locate their faith you might realize that they are not even saved. Therefore, listen to the leading of the Holy Spirit.

▶ **Praying for a young child:** Be sensitive, as the child might be afraid of strangers and in fear of being touched by you. Don't be forceful or make a big deal about it, but rather let the parent lay hands on the child. If you desire, you can lay your hand on the parent's back as a point of contact, transferring the healing power of the Lord.

▶ **Praying for an adult:** Don't assume everyone is familiar with the laying on of hands and the anointing of oil; though family members may agree with you coming, they may not be familiar with this practice. Be open and ask if they are familiar with what the Bible says about laying hands on the sick and anointing with oil. Show them the Scripture and ask if that would be alright with each of them, especially with the one who is sick.

Is anyone among you sick? Let him call for the elders of the church, and let them pray over him, anointing him with oil in the name of the Lord.
James 5:14 NKJV

Regardless of whether you know the person who is sick, inquire of the Holy Spirit if you should ask to be alone with this person. What they say to you in private can make a world of difference. Even if you are a stranger to them, they might open up. I've experienced this on several ocassions. You may even have an opportunity to lead them to the Lord if in a private setting. Whatever the case, don't be overly aggressive.

In some cases where the sick individual has personally invited you to come, ask if they want to meet with you privately. If so, ask how they would like you to handle the situation if there are other visitors there. Here are some suggestions of what you might say in the presence of visitors:

1. *"Shall I come back at a later time?"* At this point, sometimes the visitors will excuse themselves and take the hint that you wanted to be alone.

2. Or the one who is sick can ask the visitors if they mind going down to the coffee shop for a little while.

The patient might truly desire to be with you privately. You don't want to miss this opportunity because you are there on Kingdom business.

- *Woman praying for another woman:* Women are usually very comfortable having you hold their hand when praying, and of course, you can lay your hand upon her forehead as you anoint her with oil. Most women are huggers, but if you don't know this person, be sensitive to the Holy Spirit. You might ask, *"May I give you a hug?"* Also, be sensitive if they have any medical equipment attached to them.

- *Woman praying for a man:* It's always more appropriate to have two women together or a husband and wife team. One can place his/her hand upon his forehead to anoint with oil, and the other on the opposite side of the bed can place his/her hand upon his shoulder. Usually there is no hugging.

- *Woman praying for an elderly gentleman:* In this type of setting, it isn't always necessary that you go as a team. You can lay your hand upon his forehead and anoint with oil. I have found that sometimes an elderly gentleman is comfortable with you holding his hand. You might ask, *"Would you like me to hold your hand?"* This can reflect that of a father/daughter encounter. Usually hugging is not recommended unless you are very familiar with this person.

- *Man praying for another man:* You may lay your hand upon his forehead to anoint with oil. Often times with men you might ask, *"Would you like to join hands?"*

- *Men praying for a woman:* It is always more appropriate to have two men together or a husband and wife team. One can lay his hand upon her forehead and anoint her with oil, while the other on the opposite side of the bed can place his/her hand upon her shoulder. Or, she may be more comfortable with you holding her hand. You might ask, *"May I hold your hand?"* Hugging is not recommended unless you are very familiar with this person, and there are two of you in the room.

■ *Man praying for an elderly woman:* In this type of setting, it isn't always necessary that you go in as a team. You can lay your hand upon her forehead and anoint her with oil. You may even want to ask, *"May I hold your hand?"* She may look upon you like a son and desire to receive a hug.

■ *Praying for someone who is unconscious:* An unconscious person can hear, so always be aware of this and be careful of what you say. Be sensitive to the family members who have invited you. Be open and ask if they are familiar with what the Bible says about laying hands on the sick and anointing with oil. Show them the Scripture and ask if that would be alright with them.

In every situation, be sensitive to the leading of the Holy Spirit and of any medical equipment attached to the patient.

Chapter 7

Road Map for Salvation and Praying for the Sick

Since I have mentioned salvation in several of the previous chapters, I want to share with you something that was very helpful when I was first learning to witness. I was insecure thinking I wouldn't remember the right Scriptures or where to find them. Then I realized I only needed to remember one Scripture; John 3:16. Here is the process I used.

1. Begin with John 3:16 in your Bible and at the bottom of the page write the next Scripture reference you want to go to: Romans 3:23. This now creates a road map.

2. At Romans 3:23, go to the bottom of the page and write the next Scripture reference: Romans 6:23.

3. Follow your road map to Romans 6:23 and write

the next Scripture reference: Romans 10:9-10

4. Follow your road map to Romans 10:9-10

You are now ready to pray with them to receive salvation. You might want to share this Scripture after they pray, reassuring them of their salvation.

> *I write these things to you who believe in the name of the Son of God so that you may know that you have eternal life. This is the confidence we have in approaching God: that if we ask anything according to his will, he hears us. And if we know that he hears us, whatever we ask, we know that we have what we asked of him.*
>
> I John 5:13-15 NIV

You can use this same method for other situations or use a 3x5 card kept in the front of your Bible as a reference. Here are other road maps.

1. Those with no knowledge of healing: From John 3:16, build your road map to Isaiah 53:4-5 and then I Peter 2:24, Matthew 8:17, Matthew 18:18-19 and James 5:14.

2. Those who feel unworthy to receive: From John 3:16 to Romans 8:34-36 and I John 1:9. Once they see the truth of God's love and forgiveness, you can share the healing Scriptures with them.

3. Healing Scriptures: Begin with John 3:16 and proceed to Isaiah 53:4-5.

The following is a list of other Scriptures you can select from for healing.

Isaiah 54:17	Proverbs 4:20-23
Isaiah 58:8	Joel 3:10
Psalm 103:2-5	Matthew 18:18-19
Psalm 118:17	I Peter 2:24

4. Baptism of the Holy Spirit: I'm including this just for you to have available. If this person is not familiar with the Baptism of the Holy Spirit you might explain its importance. Some verses to share are:

Romans 8:26	He perfects our prayers
Jude 20	He gives us inner strength
John 16:13	He gives us guidance

The following is a list of other Scriptures you can use for receiving the infilling of the Holy Spirit.

Luke 7:9-11	John 14:16-17
Acts 1:8 & 2:1-4	Mark 11:24

Guidelines - Praying for the Sick

Chapter 8

Marilyn's Testimony: Healed of Cancer

From my early years of attending Sunday school, two Scriptures were engrafted into my heart: Psalm 73:1, *God is good* and I John 4:8, *God is love.* I simply believed that God was a good God to me personally and that He loved me. I had become unshakable from this truth.

However, after attending church for 28 years, I had never heard a single teaching on the subject of healing, nor that Jesus healed today. I also had never heard a single healing testimony, but I was still grounded in the assurance of God's love and goodness towards me.

At the age of 28, I became very sick with cancer of the appendix which is very rare. Because it was so rare, the doctors were not able to find the cause of my sickness. After being ill for about 5 months and continually getting worse, I was admitted back into the hospital, this time for exploratory surgery.

Shortly after being admitted, I was prepped for surgery. However, because the doctors were unable to detect what was wrong with me, I was given a wrong procedure. This in turn put pressure on my appendix causing it to begin to rupture. Suddenly it felt as though a volcano was about to erupt on the inside of me. I managed to get out of bed, but found it very difficult to walk. Struggling, I finally managed to get into the restroom.

Once there, I saw something that caught my attention. It was a small red button on the wall with the words *EMERGENCY* written underneath. At that point I knew something was seriously wrong and I needed to call for help. As I reached out to touch the emergency button, the Lord, in all His love and goodness, intervened in my life.

In my attempt to touch the button, my finger bounced away. Uncertain as to what just happened, I reached out a second time to hit the button, and a second time my finger bounced away. It was like, *boing, boing*! Again not understanding what was happening, I made a third attempt to hit the button.

However, this time I reached out with my whole hand. At that point, I came in contact with a wall that was between my hand and the button. It was a wall I could feel, but could not see...an invisible wall. Suddenly, I was uncertain as to what was happening. An invisible wall did not compute with me.

As soon as I had that thought about an invisible wall, I heard an audible voice three separate times.

"Your time is up! Under your present condition you are destined to die."

"Your life has been removed from the hands of mankind. Your condition is now beyond the help of the medical profession."

Then I heard the words from the *Gospel of John* 14:6, *"I am the way, the truth and the life. Through Me you can change your destiny, you don't have to die."* With great assurance, I knew this was the Lord speaking to me.

Without a moment of hesitation I responded, *"Lord, I have read that Scripture so many times and I thought You were always talking about spiritual salvation only. But Lord, I know I am saved. I remember the day I was born again. So You must be talking about a physical salvation, like healing. I don't know one thing about healing, but I do know that You love me and if You have a healing for me, then I take it."*

I wasn't sure what to expect, however, my pain greatly intensified. Fear wanted to grip me, but somehow I knew not to give place to fear. I only wanted to give place to His love.

Pressing my stomach with my left hand and thinking that I was possibly going to pass out or fall to the floor because of the excruciating pain, I reached out with my right hand to grab hold of the support bar on the wall. As I looked up towards Heaven, everything within me cried out, *"God help me, help me, help me."*

Suddenly, the Scripture in Isaiah 41:13 came alive, *"For I the Lord thy God will take hold of thy right hand, fear not, I will help thee."*

Immediately, I felt the hand of the Lord taking hold of my right hand. Quickly turning my head towards my right hand, I couldn't see Him, but I felt His hand squeezing mine as though He was saying, *"Yes, it's Me."* It was a gentle squeeze, but there was so much authority in His touch. It was at that moment I began to experience agape love like I had never experienced in all my life. He was revealing not just His love for me, but for all humanity. There are no words to describe the magnitude of His love for us. It is indescribable, immeasurable and never-ending.

In a moment's time, heat began to flow into my hand from His. This heat began to rise up my arm. It was almost like watching mercury rising in a thermometer. When the heat reached my shoulder, the best way to describe it is the *motion of lift* continued and the Lord lifted my spirit out of my body.

Once again, there are no words to describe the glory of such an experience. I was so aware that my spirit was out of my body and I had been removed from all the distractions and pain of the flesh. There was also a great awareness of being in oneness with my Lord. It was absolutely glorious. It was at this time the Lord began to teach me about healing and the power of the cross.

The Lord opened my eyes to see into the spirit realm, enabling me to see my spirit, and for the first time I realized I am a spirit being. Then laying hands on my spirit and saying, *"Lord, it's my spirit that loves you. It's my spirit that is born again."* After 28 years of church attendance, I had never been taught this. Now I received the revelation that I am a spirit being with a soul, and that my spirit and soul are housed in my physical body. My eyes were suddenly looking down into my hospital room to see my body. This was an amazing experience. I witnessed the suffering of my body, but I, *spirit man*, could feel no pain. Realizing I wasn't sick, but rather the house (physical body) I lived in was sick.

Continually looking back and forth from my spirit to my body, I grasped the true meaning of what Jesus did on the cross: *"Himself took our infirmities and bare our sicknesses." (Matthew 8:17).* He took our sickness that we might have healing and walk in divine health.

I don't know how long I was in this state with the Lord, but when He finished teaching me about healing, He released the grip of my hand. Instantly, I was back in my body; I took a small breath, but could feel no pain. I took a little deeper breath and again there was no pain. Then a deep breath and still no pain. Placing my hands on my stomach, I whispered, *"I'm healed! I'm healed!"*

Though not knowing yet what I was healed from, I was truly aware of being touched by the love of God and that something marvelous had happened. My only desire was to return to my bed and worship the Lord. I didn't want to talk to anyone, but only to embrace what had happened. It seemed that talking would contaminate the moment.

A short time later someone came to take me to the operating room. Not knowing how to explain my beautiful encounter with the Lord, I said nothing. From surgery I was taken to the recovery room where my doctor came to see me.

He was an elderly, semi-retired gentleman who was a very compassionate person with an excellent bedside manner. As he held my hand, he began to speak about the operation.

"Marilyn, something must have happened to you prior to surgery. During the operation I found cancer, but it wasn't attached to you. I didn't have to cut anything to remove the cancer." He repeated, *"The cancer wasn't attached to you.*

Therefore, you don't need any chemotherapy or radiation treatment." He then repeated several times, *"Something must have happened. All systems were go for ruptured appendix, but something stopped it before the operation."*

He went on to say, *"Because of the procedure you were given prior to surgery, your appendix should have ruptured. If that would have happened, the cancer would have spread throughout your entire system and it would have killed you. You would have died within less than two weeks and it would have been a very painful death. But something stopped it. I have never seen anything like this before."* Again he repeated, *"Something must have happened to you before the operation."*

Later, when I was alone, I once again I heard the voice of the Lord whispering my name.

"Marilyn, when I was holding your hand, I was also holding back your appendix from rupturing so the doctor could go in and remove the cancer in its entirety, because I wanted you to know exactly what I did for you."

What a joy to experience the faithfulness and love of the Lord through the power of His resurrection. He still performs miracles today!

Epilogue

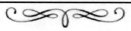

God's Medicine

Healing has been provided through the Atonement.

> *Surely He has borne our griefs and carried our sorrows; yet we esteemed Him stricken, smitten by God, and afflicted. But He was wounded for our transgressions, He was bruised for our iniquities; the chastisement for our peace was upon Him, and by His stripes we are healed.*
>
> Isaiah 53:4-5

Many times you must first deal with the spirit of fear before those suffering with sickness and disease can release their faith to be healed.

> *For God has not given us a spirit of fear, but of power and of love and of a sound mind.*
>
> 2 Timothy 1:7

▪ HEALING SCRIPTURES ▪

For I am the LORD who heals you.
                                                Exodus 15:26 NKJV

So you shall serve the LORD your God, and He will bless your bread and your water. And I will take sickness away from the midst of you.
                                                Exodus 23:25 NKJV

And the Lord will take away from you all sickness.
                                                Deuteronomy 7:15 AMP

Bless (affectionately, gratefully praise) the Lord, O my soul, and forget not [one of] all His benefits. Who forgives [every one of] all your iniquities, Who heals [each one of] all your diseases, Who redeems your life from the pit and corruption (destruction).
                                                Psalm 103:2-4 AMP

He sent His word and healed them, and delivered them from their destructions.
                                                Psalm 107:20 NKJV

Again I say to you that if two of you agree on earth concerning anything that they ask, it will be done for them by My Father in heaven.
                                                Matthew 18:19 NKJV

Is anyone among you sick? Let him call for the elders of the church, and let them pray over him, anointing him with oil in the name of the Lord. And the prayer of faith will save the sick, and the Lord will raise him up. And if he has committed sins, he will be forgiven.

James 5:14-15 KJV

No weapon [sickness or disease] formed against you shall prosper.

Isaiah 54:17 NKJV

Then shall your light break forth like the morning, and your healing (your restoration and the power of a new life) shall spring forth speedily.

Isaiah 58:8 AMP

He Himself took our infirmities and bore our sicknesses.

Matthew 8:17b NKJV

Who Himself bore our sins in His own body on the tree, that we, having died to sins, might live for righteousness, by whose stripes you were healed.

1 Peter 2:24 NKJV

▪ SPECIFIC HEALING SCRIPTURES ▪

▪ Animal Bites and Attacks ▪

For you will have a covenant with the stones of the field, and the wild animals will be at peace with you.
Job 5:23 NIV

Deliver my life from the sword, my precious life from the power of the dogs. Rescue me from the mouth of the lions; save me from the horns of the wild oxen.
Psalm 22:20-21 NIV

▪ Arthritis, Bone Cancer, Osteoporosis ▪

The LORD will guide you continually, and satisfy your soul in drought, and strengthen your bones; You shall be like a watered garden, and like a spring of water, whose waters do not fail.
Isaiah 58:11 NKJV

▪ Blood Diseases and Disorders ▪
(AIDS, Leukemia, Diabetes, Blood Pressure, Abnormal Bleeding)

And when I passed by you and saw you struggling in your own blood, I said to you in your blood, 'Live!' Yes, I said to you in your blood, 'Live!'
Ezekiel 16:6 NKJV

For I will cleanse their blood that I have not cleansed: for the LORD dwelleth in Zion.

Joel 3:21 KJV

▪ Bones ▪

The righteous man may have many troubles, but the LORD delivers him from them all; He protects all his bones, not one of them will be broken.

Psalm 34:19-20 NIV

Be not wise in your own eyes; fear the LORD and depart from evil. It will be... strength to your bones.

Proverbs 3:7-8 NKJV

▪ Burns ▪

Then his flesh is renewed like a child's, it is restored as in the days of his youth.

Job 33:25 NIV

▪ Cancer and Life-Threatening Diseases ▪

He sent His word and healed them, and delivered them from their destructions.

Psalm 107:20 NKJV

For the law of the Spirit of life in Christ Jesus hath made me free from the law of sin and death.

Romans 8:2 KJV

▪ Child Bearing ▪

No one shall suffer miscarriage or be barren in your land; I will fulfill the number of your days.

Exodus 23:26 KJV

Thou shalt know also that thy seed shall be great, and thine offspring as the grass of the earth.

Job 5:25 KJV

▪ Eyes and Ears ▪

Then will the eyes of the blind be opened and the ears of the deaf unstopped.

Isaiah 35:5 NIV

The LORD gives sight to the blind.

Psalm 146:8 NIV

▪ Feet ▪

He will keep the feet of his saints, and the wicked shall be silent in darkness; for by strength shall no man prevail.

1 Samuel 2:9 KJV

Forty years You sustained them in the wilderness, They lacked nothing; Their clothes did not wear out and their feet did not swell.

Nehemiah 9:21 KJV

▪ Joints ▪

Strengthen the feeble hands, steady the knees that give way.

Isaiah 35:3 NIV

▪ Lame ▪

The Sovereign LORD is my strength; He makes my feet like the feet of a deer, He enables me to go on the heights.

Habakkuk 3:19 NIV

And the blind and the lame came to him in the temple; and he healed them.

Matthew 21:14 KJV

▪ Long Life ▪

You shall come to the grave at a full age, as a sheaf of grain ripens in its season.

Job 5:26 KJV

He shall call upon me, and I will answer him: I will be with him in trouble; I will deliver him, and honor him. With long life will I satisfy him, and show him my salvation.

Psalm 91:15-16 KJV

For by me thy days shall be multiplied, and the years of thy life shall be increased.

Proverbs 9:11 KJV

▪ Mute ▪

Then will the lame leap like a deer, and the mute tongue shout for joy.

Isaiah 35:6 NIV

▪ Osteoporosis (see arthritis) ▪

The LORD lifts me up when I am bowed down...

Psalm 146:8 NIV

▪ Plagues and Epidemics ▪

Surely He will save you from the fowler's snare and from the deadly pestilence.

Psalm 91:3 NIV

There shall no evil befall me, nor shall any plague or calamity come near my dwelling; for He gives His angels charge over me, to accompany, defend and preserve me in all my ways of obedience and service.

Psalm 91:10-11 AMP

▪ Poison ▪

They will pick up snakes with their hands; and

when they drink deadly poison, it will not hurt them at all.

Mark 16:18 NIV

I have given you authority to trample on snakes and scorpions and to overcome all the power of the enemy; nothing will harm you.

Luke 10:19 NIV

▪ Sores ▪

I will restore you to health and heal your wounds, declares the LORD.

Jeremiah 30:17 NIV

▪ Strength ▪

But they that wait upon the LORD shall renew their strength; they shall mount up with wings as eagles; they shall run, and not be weary; and they shall walk, and not faint.

Isaiah 40:31 KJV

Let the weak say, I am strong.

Joel 3:10 KJV

▪ Terminal Cases ▪

No weapon that is formed against thee shall prosper;

and every tongue that shall rise against thee in judgment thou shalt condemn. This is the heritage of the servants of the LORD, and their righteousness is of me, saith the LORD.

Isaiah 54:17 KJV

I will not die, but live and proclaim what the Lord has done.

Psalm 118:17 NIV

Personal Thoughts, Prayers and Victories

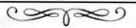

Personal Coaching

*As a lighthouse is to a lost ship at sea guiding her to the shore,
I am here to guide you into the light of God's Word
and bring you to a place of divine healing.*

Dear Ambassador,

If you're ministering to someone who would like to have personal contact with me and receive information about personal coaching for healing, you may give them my email address:

marilynneubauer@gmail.com

Dr. Marilyn Neubauer

About the Author

After receiving a miraculous healing from a rare form of cancer, her near death experience with malaria and the miraculous disappearance of a large tumor, Dr. Neubauer began to teach on the healing power of God.

As an international speaker and author, her practical message of the Gospel of faith and her revelation of Jesus as the Healer has opened an international platform throughout the world. She has been embraced in denominational and independent churches, Bible schools and conferences. Her message embraces Triumphant Living for the total man: spirit, soul and body.

Dr. Marilyn Neubauer has received an Honorary Doctor of Divinity degree from Cambridge Theological Seminary.

Other books written by
Dr. Marilyn Neubauer

Instructions from the Great Physician
We choose life and health
as we follow God's instructions.
(Also available in Spanish and German)

My Daily Delight in the Lord
A book of praise and daily confessions.
(Also available in Spanish and German)

Welcome to the Family
An excellent study guide for a
membership class or a new believer's class.
Also excellent for cell groups bringing
the mature saints back to the basics.
(Book and workbook)
(Also available in Spanish and German)

What's My Next Step? I'm a New Believer
A strong emphasis on the importance
of the local church for the new believer.
(Also available in Spanish)

Purchase your copy here:

Marilyn Neubauer Ministries
P.O. Box 4664
Oceanside, CA 92052
www.marilynneubauer.com
marilynneubauer@gmail.com